| DATE DUE | | | |
|---|---|---|---|
| | | | |
| | | | |
| | | | |
| | | | |
| | | | |
| | | | |
| | | | |
| | | | |
| | | | |
| | | | |
| | | | |
| | | | |

GARETH STEVENS
VITAL SCIENCE
*Physical Science*

# HISTORY
# OF SCIENCE

by Philip Steele
Science curriculum consultant: Suzy Gazlay, M.A.,
science curriculum resource teacher

GARETH**STEVENS**
**GS**
PUBLISHING
A Member of the WRC Media Family of Companies

Please visit our Web site at: www.garethstevens.com
For a free color catalog describing Gareth Stevens Publishing's
list of high-quality books and multimedia programs, call
1-800-542-2595 (USA) or 1-800-387-3178 (Canada).
Gareth Stevens Publishing's fax: (414) 332-3567.

**Library of Congress Cataloging-in-Publication Data**

Steele, Philip, 1948-
    History of science / Philip Steele.
      p. cm. — (Gareth Stevens vital science. Physical science)
    Includes bibliographical references and index.
    ISBN-13: 978-0-8368-8086-1 (lib. bdg.)
    ISBN-13: 978-0-8368-8095-3 (softcover)
    1. Science—History. I. Title.
    Q125.S7424    2007
    509—dc22                   2006033447

This edition first published in 2007 by
**Gareth Stevens Publishing**
A Member of the WRC Media Family of Companies
330 West Olive Street, Suite 100
Milwaukee, WI 53212 USA

This edition copyright © 2007 by Gareth Stevens, Inc.

Editors: Rebecca Hunter, Amy Bauman
Designer: Melissa Valuch
Photo researcher: Rachel Tisdale
Gareth Stevens editorial direction: Mark Sachner
Gareth Stevens editor: Carol Ryback
Gareth Stevens art direction: Tammy West
Gareth Stevens graphic design: Dave Kowalski
Gareth Stevens production: Jessica Yanke and Robert Kraus

Illustrations by Stefan Chabluk
Photo credits: CFW Images: 9 (Chris Fairclough); 24 (EASI-Images/Edward Parker);
CORBIS: cover (Massimo Listri); 6, 25 (DK Limited); Getty Images: 4 (Hulton Archive); 5
(Jim Cummins); 7 (Robert Frerck); 8 (Babylonian School/The Bridgeman Art library); 10
(Hulton Archive); 11 (Italian School/The Bridgeman Art Library); 18 (Yale Joel/Time Life
Pictures); 27 (Mansell/Time Life Pictures); 31 (Hulton Archive); 34 (Hulton Archive);
39 (Sylvain Grandadam); 40 (Geoff Robins/AFP); 42 (Michael Smith); 42 (Sion Touhig);
Istockphoto: 12 (Jan Tyler); 13 (Christine Balderas); 17 (Rob Friedman); 19 (Monika
Wisniewska); 28 (Michael Fernahl); 29 (Federico Arnao); 36 (Jan Kaliciak); 37 top
(Matthew Gough); 41 (Matthew Ludgate); Library of Congress: 15, 16, 20, 21, 22, 26,
30, 32; (U.S. Office of War Information) 35; NASA title page: 14 (ESA/STScI); 33, 37
bottom, 38 (TRW/NASA-MSFC); Photodisc: 23 top.

Printed in Canada

1 2 3 4 5 6 7 8 9 10 10 09 08 07 06

# TABLE OF CONTENTS

Words that appear in the glossary are printed in **boldface** type the first time they appear in the text.

**Cover:** *The Alchemist's Laboratory*; a painting by Stradanus, 1570.

**Title page image:** The first Moon landing in July 1969 marked one of the greatest achievements in the history of science.

# Introduction

People have always asked questions about the world around them. How does the human body work? How far away is the Moon? Why do we see colors or hear sound? Why do things fall to the ground?

## Finding Out

Science is a way of discovering the truth. The Romans used the word *scientia*, meaning "knowledge," about two thousand years ago. In the Middle Ages, scholars called science "natural **philosophy**." By this, they meant knowledge about nature and the **universe**, about what things are made of, and about why these things behave as they do. Ideas were passed from one generation to the next, but they were rarely questioned or tested.

## Let's Investigate

The modern scientific method developed in the 1600s. Scientific method works simi-lar to a detective investigation that takes nothing for granted. The process starts wit asking questions. Tests, or experiments, ma be set up to provide answers.

Each stage of the investigation must be based only on **evidence**, which is gathere by observing what happens, and by measu ing and recording the results. The case can be proven only if tests prove accurate and if the results can be repeated by someone else.

The basic tool used to carry out such work and to make scientific calculations is mathematics. Mathematics is a sort of un versal language used by scientists. It can describe precisely number, shape, movement, structure, and how things happen.

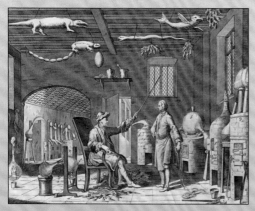

A scientist directs his assistant during experiments in a laboratory of the 1740s.

## PHILOSOPHY

"Philosophy is written in this grand book the Universe, which stands continually open to our gaze... It is written in the language of mathematics."

Galileo Galilei (1564-1642)

## Studying Everything

Modern science embraces many subjects. Many of these fall into three main categories—earth sciences, life sciences, and physical sciences—each of which includes many branches and specialties. Physical sciences, for example, include such sciences as physics (the study of matter, energy, and their relationships) and chemistry (the study of what things are made of and how they react with each other). Biology (the study of all living things) is a life science, while geology (the study of Earth and its rocks) is an Earth science. Some sciences may belong to more than one branch.

Science is closely linked to **technology**, the way in which we use our knowledge to improve our lives. "Improving our lives" can mean making things—from frozen pizzas and skyscrapers to mobile phones and spacecraft—improving them, or even improving the way they are made. Sometimes, people learn how to make something first and then determine the science that makes it possible. Sometimes the scientific discovery comes first, and this leads to new inventions.

### Why History?

Science affects every part of our daily lives, but why do we need to know about science in the past? It is important for us to understand how ideas developed over time. This helps us see how we might solve problems that puzzle us today or to see where people have gone wrong in the past. Looking at the past to see how scientists have struggled to discover the truth is very exciting, but looking at the past is also a key to the future.

The science we learn at school today is often the result of hundreds of years of research, experimentation, failure, and success.

# Ancient Questions

Prehistoric humans were successful because they were intelligent. They may not have had access to the vast amounts of information available to us today, but their personal brain power was much the same as ours, and it helped them survive.

## Magic and Myths

Early peoples were curious about the world around them, and they became skillful makers of tools and weapons. They asked important questions. Why does night follow day? Why did the Sun sometimes disappear in what we now know was an **eclipse**? Why do people die? What is fire? How does an arrow fly and fall?

When people could find no obvious explanation, they looked for answers in magic or in stories, called **myths**, which tried to explain the event. They also developed beliefs in spirits and gods and tried to control their world by ceremonies, or **rituals**, that pleased or honored those spirits. Why did thunder crash and lightning fork? Because a god was angry. What could

About 4,000 years ago, Stonehenge in Britain may have been used to mark the midsummer sunrise.

e done if there was a **drought**? Dancing ight please the gods, who would then ake it rain. Why did people get sick? — ecause evil spirits had taken hold of them.

## rial and Error

rehistoric humans were able to learn from xperience and observation. For example, ey tried eating plants and soon found out hich were safe and which were poison- us. They learned that certain roots or erbs could cure illnesses. They developed ols to help them hunt and build things. hey learned to prepare colored paints om **minerals**, charcoal, and grease. The ictures they made on the walls of their ves often lasted for tens of ousands of years.

Prehistoric people learned successfully hunt wild ani- als by observing their behav- r. They learned how to haul d push, how to use a lever lift heavy objects, and how roll these objects along on gs. They learned how things oat on water and how to prove the flight of a spear. hey learned how to make d control fire and to cook food. This ability to learn and change behavior is the basis of all science.

## Stone Age Inventions

From the activities of "cave people," we can see the origins of modern science and technology. Humans used their discoveries about materials to make clever inventions. In about 50,000 B.C., people in western Asia and Europe were carving little lamps from stone and using animal fat as fuel. The earliest pottery was probably made in Japan, and has been dated to about 14,000 B.C. In 12,000 B.C., peoples in northeast Africa were using grindstones to make flour from wild grass seeds.

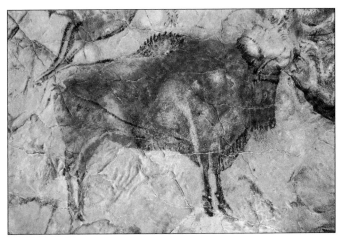

This cave painting from Spain probably dates back to 12,000 B.C. The animal is drawn accurately.

## Farming and Science

The earliest farming probably took place in the river valleys of western Asia, beginning about 12,000 years ago. Wild animals such as goats, sheep, and cows were kept in herds. These animals were used for food, milk, hides, and fibers, such as wool. Wild seeds were gathered and then planted for food crops, such as wheat. Farming led directly to all kinds of scientific advances. Gradually, farmers began to experiment with breeding and learned how to select only those animals and plant seeds that would produce the best offspring or crops.

This 2,600 year-old world map shows lands around the city of Babylon, in Mesopotamia.

## Calendars and Stars

Through the centuries, farmers became mor skilled. They studied how rivers flooded and kept track of sowing and harvests times. Fiv thousand years ago, the ancient Egyptians learned to predict the yearly flood of the Nile River by observing the rising of the star called Sirius. They called it "Sopdet," and believed that the star was a goddess. Their priests devised calendars to measure the passing seasons.

Early peoples from all over the world studie the apparent movements of the Sun, Moon, and stars across the sky, founding the scienc of **astronomy**. In some cases, they raised stones or built monuments that served as primitive viewing spots, or **observatories**. For example, the massive stones at Stonehenge, in southern England, were aligned to movements of the Sun. The stones were arranged sometime between 3200 and 1500 B.C.

## Useful Sums

Regular supplies of homegrown food made it possible for people to live in towns and cities—Jericho, in Palestine, is more than ter thousand years old. Building projects of this size called for the ability to calculate and measure accurately as well as the ability to **survey**, or examine, the land to determine the best sites. Merchants and tax collectors also needed to count, to determine the valu of goods or land and to keep records of business transactions.

## Experiments with Metal

Humans soon learned how to experiment with the materials they found around them. Clay could be fired to make hard bricks and pottery. **Ores**, which are rocks containing metals, could be heated in a furnace—a process called **smelting**. Molten metal could then be removed from the rock and poured into molds or hammered into tools and weapons. By 3000 B.C., workers in western Asia had learned to mix metals to make **alloys**. One alloy, bronze, is made by combining tin and copper. Iron, a pure metal, was being worked by 1400 B.C. By changing materials through heating and hammering, humans were creating new technologies based on chemical processes.

## Around the World

Scientific advances occurred in different parts of the world at different times. Many important early discoveries were made in Mesopotamia (ancient Iraq), between about 3500 and 500 B.C. This is the valley region located between the Tigris and Euphrates Rivers. It was here that writing and num-

Alloys of copper have been used in Asia for more than eight thousand years. Metalworking taught people about the properties of different materials.

bers first developed, that hours were first divided into sixty minutes, and that the **constellations** (groups of stars as seen from Earth) were recorded.

**Did You Know?**

**PYRAMID MATH**

Giant tombs called pyramids were constructed in Egypt between about 3667 and 1750 b.c. To create these huge structures, the Egyptians not only used technology, but also used mathematics. They knew how to determine the area of a rectangle or a circle and could calculate the volume of a cylinder or a pyramid.

# Seekers of Knowledge

The word "philosophy" comes from a Greek word, meaning "love of wisdom." The ancient Greeks are a people who settled many lands around the Mediterranean Sea. They loved to argue about ideas. They began to use reason in their attempt to explain the workings of the universe, rather than referring to magic or myths.

## What Was Everything Made Of?

The scientist Thales was one of the first Greeks to look beyond magic and myth to help explain the world. Thales lived from about 624 to 546 B.C. He was fascinated by astronomy and **geometry**. He wanted to know what all matter was made of. The answer, he decided, was water. He was wrong, but others followed his quest for the truth.

In about 450 B.C., another Greek, Empedocles, claimed that matter was made up of four basic **elements**—earth, air, fire, and water. Wrong again. But just a few years later, a thinker named Leucippus and his pupil, Democritus, came very near the truth, when they suggested that matter was made of tiny particles that could not be divided. They called them **atoms**.

## The Beauty of Ideas

One of the greatest Greek thinkers was Aristotle, who founded a school of philosophy in about 335 B.C. He loved science as much for the beauty of its ideas as for its practical uses. He was not always correct, but he observed animal and plant life with

The work of Pythagoras was still being studied in Europe in the Middle Ages.

### NATURE

"Nature does nothing without purpose..."

Aristotle (384-322 B.C.)

reat care. He studied motion, too, and was ne first to use the word "*physics*."

Many Greeks were brilliant mathematiians. Pythagoras, in about 530 B.C., was bsessed with numbers and fascinated by eometry. He studied the arithmetic of usical notes. He was a bit cranky, howev-r, and held many strange views, such as not llowing his followers to eat beans!

### Eureka!"

rchimedes, who lived from bout 287 to 211 B.C., was an nventor and a brilliant mathe-natician, too. He was an expert n the physics of water. One day, e was asked by King Hiero to ind out whether the royal rown was made of pure gold r mixed with cheaper metals. ying in the bath, Archimedes ealized that he could figure it ut by comparing the amount f water **displaced** by the crown vith the amount of water lisplaced by an equal weight f pure gold. The story goes that he was o excited at solving this problem that

Pliny the Elder (A.D. 23–79) was a Roman who studied nature and science. He died investigating the eruption of the Mount Vesuvius volcano near Pompeii.

he ran naked down the street, shouting *Eureka*!" ("I have found it!")

## RIGHT THE FIRST TIME!

• In about 260 B.C., Aristarchus claimed that Earth and the other planets traveled around the Sun. He was correct, but few people believed him. It was more than 1,800 years before this theory was put forward again.

• In about 250 B.C., Eratosthenes tried to figure out the distance around Earth at the poles by comparing shadows cast by the Sun in different places. Incredibly, he was accurate to within just 252 miles (406 kilometers).

Roman science and technology are perfectly matched in this aqueduct, the Pont du Gard near Nimes, in southern France. It is almost two thousand years old.

## Greek Medicine

Greek doctors were pioneers of modern medicine. They observed a patient's **symptoms** and made careful conclusions, or **diagnoses**. Doctors today still try to base their professional behavior on that of Hippocrates, who is said to have founded a medical school on the island of Cos (in what is now Greece) in about 430 B.C. Historians now think that the teachings of "Hippocrates" may in fact have been the work of not just one, but several people.

## Roman Technology

Greek science was accepted by the Romans, who 1,900 years ago ruled a vast area of Europe, north Africa, and western Asia. The Romans were brilliant engineers. They built fine roads, bridges, temples, and high-rise aqueducts (water channels).

## Medieval Europe

Greek science was also accepted in Europe during the Middle Ages. This thousand-year period followed the end of Roman power in A.D. 476. Aristotle's teachings were followed by the Christian churches and few people questioned them. If Aristotle said that the Sun traveled around Earth, then so it did.

A few medieval scholars were more original in their approach to science. English bishop Robert Grosseteste, (1175–1253), called for careful testing and checking of theories, as in modern science. He himself investigated light, rainbows, tides, mathematics, astronomy, and science in general.

# Q&A

## NO SENSE OF HUMOR?

• In ancient Greece and during the Middle Ages, doctors believed that good health depended on the balance of four fluids or "humors" present in the human body. The four included blood, black bile, yellow bile, and phlegm.

• The humors were linked to mood, seasons, humidity, and body temperature.

• "Cures" for poor health included being wrapped up in bed, drinking liquor and other fluids, being made to vomit, or having blood sucked from the body by leeches! Leeches are still used today to help clean wounds.

## Chinese and Indian Science

Asia was the site of some of the most interesting scientific activities in the Middle Ages. The Chinese made great advances in the study of motion, **magnetism**, geology, chemistry, mathematics, and medicine. For example, they knew that blood circulated around the body hundreds of years before European scientists discovered that fact. Chinese inventions included compasses, paper, printing, gunpowder, and ships' rudders.

Between 400 and 1100, India also saw a great age of metal sciences, mathematics, medicine, and **botany**. Indian astronomer and mathematician Brahmagupta (598–670) studied in this era of growth. Among his contributions is a better understanding of the number zero.

## Arab and Persian Science

European, Chinese, and Indian science were all studied closely by Arab and Persian (Iranian) scholars during the Middle Ages. They, too, followed Aristotle's ideas.

Many were brilliant doctors, geographers, astronomers, and mathematicians—"algebra," in fact, is an Arabic word. They studied light and **optics** and calculated the height of Earth's **atmosphere** (the layer of gases surrounding the planet). Great scientists such as "Avicenna" (Ibn Sina, 980–1037) and "Averroes" (Ibn Rushd, 1126–1198) were famous across Europe.

The earliest versions of the magnetic compass were known in China in the fourth century B.C.

13

# CHAPTER 3

# New Science

In the 1500s, renewed interest in "natural philosophy" developed in European universities. More and more people were now ready to question the age-old theories of science that few had challenged for so long.

## Sun, Moon, and Planets

Nicolaus Copernicus lived in Poland from 1473 to 1543. He studied mathematics, medicine, and astronomy. The more he read about explanations for movements of the Sun and Earth, the more he was sure that most ancient Greeks had gotten it wrong. Copernicus used mathematics to show how planets orbit the Sun, rotating as they move. These ideas were published in the year he died. Many people were shocked and angry. If humans were God's most important creation, then surely Earth had to be at the center of the universe!

## Observation and Data

So how *did* the universe work? That was the big question. In 1576, astronomer Tycho Brahe (1546–1601) built an observatory in Denmark. He did not believe the theories of Copernicus, but he wanted answers. For

Pictures of deep space would not be possible without today's high-powered telescopes.

twenty years, Brahe watched the skies, precisely measuring the positions of the plants and hundreds of stars.

Brahe's assistant was a German astronomer and mathematician named Johannes Kepler (1571–1630). Kepler used the data Brahe had collected, studying the planets and their distance from the Sun. He realized that the planets were indeed traveling around the Sun but not in circular orbits. The paths they followed were oval, or **elliptical**.

### THE SUN

"Finally we shall place the Sun himself at the center of the Universe."

Nicolaus Copernicus (1473-1543)

## Telescope Evidence

In 1608, Dutchman Hans Lippershey (1570–1619) displayed an invention called a telescope. Lippershey's telescope was made of two glass lenses fixed in a tube. Its purpose was to make distant objects appear nearer. As light entered the tube, the first lens bent the rays and brought an image into focus. The second lens magnified it.

Italian scientist Galileo Galilei (1564–1642) used the telescope to study the skies. He now saw the evidence with his own eyes. He realized that the Milky Way, a cloudy band of light across the night sky, was actually made up of countless stars. The stars he was seeing, in fact, were other stars in our own **galaxy**. He observed details of the Moon's surface and some of the moons around the planet Jupiter. He saw reflections of sunlight from the planet Venus. His studies convinced Galileo of one thing: The planets were orbiting the Sun. Copernicus and Kepler had been right.

Galileo was a true scientist who relied on hard evidence instead of traditional ideas. He helped change our view of the universe.

## Q&A  CAN YOU HANDLE THIS PLANET?

In 1610, Galileo turned his telescope toward the planet Saturn. On either side of it, he saw strange bulging shapes, like the handles on a jug. What had he seen? Even Galileo didn't know.

In 1655, Christiaan Huygens declared that Saturn must be surrounded by a ring. In the 1800s, astronomers finally realized that Saturn was indeed surrounded by bands of particles that form many rings.

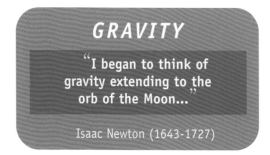

## GRAVITY

"I began to think of gravity extending to the orb of the Moon..."

Isaac Newton (1643-1727)

## Ether and Atoms

The bigger picture of the truth about the universe was beginning to appear. It was as if scientists were putting together pieces of a jigsaw puzzle, carefully assembling the evidence.

The amazing Frenchman René Descartes (1596-1650), was a philosopher and brilliant mathematician who thought that the universe worked like a huge machine. He claimed, wrongly, that an invisible swirling and whirling matter called ether must fill space.

At the same time, some researchers, such as French scientist Pierre Gassendi (1592-1655), returned to the ancient notion that all matter was made up of tiny particles called atoms. This time, this idea became more widely accepted.

## The Pull of Gravity

The greatest scientist of this new age was Isaac Newton (1643-1727). He was born in England the year that Galileo died. Legend has it that a falling apple inspired Newton to investigate the way in which objects are pulled to the ground. He realized that this attraction, called **gravity**, also works on a much larger scale in space, holding moons in orbit around their planets.

## The Science of Movement

The universe that the scientists were discovering was one that is forever in motion. All the forces of nature depend on movement. Although Aristotle had claimed that the rate at which an object falls depends on its weight, Galileo proved that if there was no **resistance** from air, all objects would fall at the same rate. He also studied the way in which objects in motion **accelerate** or change velocity (speed and direction of

Isaac Newton was a scientific genius, investigating gravity, light, and motion.

Q&A

## WHAT! NO COMPUTERS?

• In the 1600s, scientists had to do complex math problems without computers. They learned very clever ways of taking mathematical shortcuts and developed new systems of calculating.

• Both Isaac Newton and German mathematician Gottfried Leibniz (1646-1716), working separately, came up with methods for solving complicated math problems with great accuracy using a method called calculus. They also spent many years arguing over who discovered calculus first!

motion), as well as why **pendulums** swing back and forth.

In 1686, Isaac Newton completed a book that would change science forever. Its full title in English was *Mathematical Principles of Natural Philosophy*, but it was generally just called the *Principia*. In this book, Newton set out the laws of motion. A scientific "law" is a truth that applies invariably to a sequence of natural events; it explains what happens and why. Newton stated that a steadily moving object will continue to move unless a force is applied to it. He declared that the acceleration of an object depends on the object's **mass** and the force that acts upon it. He also stated that for every action, there is an equal and opposite reaction. For example, a ball that is thrown presses against the air, while the air pushes back against it.

Newton's scientific laws described motion, such as the path of a ball through the air.

## What is Light?

What is light? How does it move? Dutch scientist Christiaan Huygens (1629–1695) thought it was a form of energy that traveled in waves. He was almost right. Newton thought that light was made up of particles, and he was not entirely wrong, either. He showed how light can be bent (**refracted**) by a multisided piece of glass called a **prism** and split up into all the colors of the rainbow.

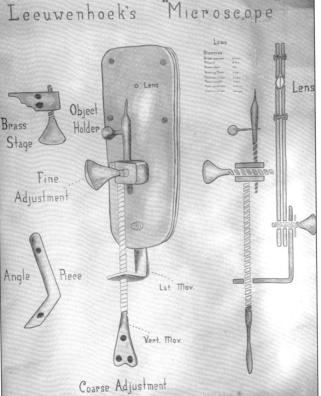

Leeuwenhoek's little microscopes could magnify up to 250 times. Specimens were placed on a central pin.

## Microscopic worlds

Another new instrument, the **microscope**, used lenses to magnify the tiniest things. It was developed by Dutch scientist Anton van Leeuwenhoek (1632–1723). He could see new miniature worlds every bit as amazing as the giant world being discovered in space today—plant **cells**, **bacteria**, the structure of blood, tiny living things in a drop of water.

## The Human Body

The microscope changed human knowledge of living things and, in particular, of the

## DO IT YOURSELF?

In the 1600s, Italy, France, and England all established official academies of science. England's academy was the Royal Society. Its Latin motto was "Nullius in verba"— which could be roughly translated as "Take no one's word for it." That summed up scientists' new attitude: Find the evidence and prove it yourself!

human body. Scientists' knowledge of this field was growing. Andreas Vesalius (1514–1564) focused on **anatomy**, which looks at the structure of living things. Like other doctors of the time, Vesalius dissected, or cut open, the human body to see how it worked. William Harvey (1578–1657) also dissected bodies. From them, he learned that the heart pumps blood through the body in a circular path.

## Alchemy or Chemistry?

Studies such as physics and biology were growing, but chemistry took a little longer to develop as a science. In the Middle Ages, chemistry was known as **alchemy**. Alchemy included many spiritual and magical ideas and could not even be called a true science. For example, alchemists tried to turn cheap metals into gold. They also sought a tonic, which they called the "elixir of life" to make people **immortal**.

It seems odd now, but in the 1600s, even scientists such as Isaac Newton and Irish scientist Robert Boyle (1627–1691) dabbled in alchemy. By experimenting with chemicals

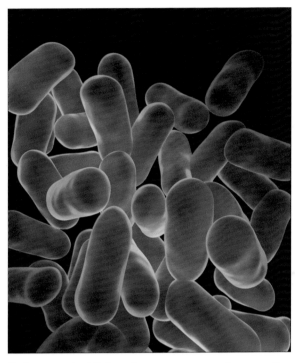

Today, a typical light microscope can easily magnify bacteria by 1,500 times!

and processes, alchemists made important discoveries. Boyle's study of metals, **acids**, and **alkalis** is regarded as the start of scientific chemistry. In 1661, Boyle introduced the modern idea of the element, which is any matter that cannot be broken down into a simpler form.

**Did You Know**

### THE EYEBALL EXPERIMENT
Isaac Newton would go to any lengths to experiment. To find out more about light and color, he once pushed a blunt needle, called a bodkin, behind his eyeball. Luckily, he did not go blind.

# CHAPTER 4

# The Age of Reason

Between 1751 and 1772, an encyclopedia was published in France. It was filled with information about everything from animals and plants to medicine and technology. The philosophers who published the encyclopedia thought that people should seek the truth by relying on reason rather than faith or the untested ideas of superstitions. Science was becoming very popular. Many amateur scientists began to collect fossils or plants; others carried out experiments with electricity.

## New Chemistry

Joseph Black (1728-1799) was a professor of chemistry in Scotland. In 1754, he identified the gas later known as carbon dioxide. In 1766, Englishman Henry Cavendish (1731-1810) discovered another gas called hydrogen.

In 1774, amateur chemist Joseph Priestley (1733-1804) discovered oxygen gas but failed to understand the part it played in the process of burning, or **combustion**.

In the eighteenth century, alchemy was replaced by a truly scientific approach. Antoine Lavoisier has been called "the father of modern chemistry."

Priestley and many people before him believed that some materials contained an invisible substance called **phlogiston**. They thought that whenever these materials burned, phlogiston was released into the air

This theory was disproved by French chemist Antoine Lavoisier (1743-1794). Lavoisier showed that burning occurred when matter is rapidly united with the new gas. Although Priestley discovered the gas, Lavoisier named it "oxygen." Lavoisier also proved that water is made up of a mixture of hydrogen and oxygen.

Scientists at last understood that Earth, water, fire, and air were not elements. Lavoisier began to make a list of elements.

## ATMOSPHERIC AIR

"Atmospheric air is not an element, that is, a simple body, but a mixture of several gases."

Antoine Lavoisier (1743-1794)

addition to oxygen and hydrogen, the known elements included phosphorus, nitrogen, zinc, mercury, and sulfur.

Lavoisier devised a new law of science: Matter may change form, as when it burns, but matter cannot be created from nothing, nor can it be destroyed. Sadly, Lavoisier's research was cut short, literally, when he was beheaded during the French Revolution.

## Measuring Heat

Scientists need to measure temperatures accurately. By the 1600s, thermometers had been invented. These were tubes that contained liquid such as colored water.

As the liquid warmed, it expanded and rose higher in the tube.

In the 1700s, scientist Gabriel Fahrenheit (1686-1736), born in Gdansk, Poland, tried using alcohol in the tube. Then he tried mercury, a liquid metal, which worked best of all.

Precise scales of temperature were set up, one by Fahrenheit and another by Swedish astronomer, Anders Celsius (1701-1744). Fahrenheit's scale set the freezing point of water at 32° and the boiling point at 212°. According to the Celsius scale, the freezing point of water was 0° and the boiling point was 100°.

**WHAT'S THAT IN THE AIR?**
When gases are heated, they rise. Two French brothers, Joseph (1740–1810) and Jacques (1745–1799) Montgolfier, used this fact to experiment with hot air balloons. In September 1783, they demonstrated their invention to the king and queen of France (above). A sheep, a duck, and a rooster were sent up in the air and safely completed a short flight.

21

# History of Science

## Electric Shocks

*Physics*, too, was making great progress in this age of reason. The subject that had everyone excited was electricity. People had been puzzled by this for more than one thousand years. Greek scientist and philosopher Thales had observed that rubbing a piece of **amber** with fur caused lighter materials such as bits of feathers or straw to cling to it. At the time, people confused that attraction—which we now know is static electricity—with magnetism. The word "electricity" comes from the Greek word for amber—"*elektron*."

In the 1600s and 1700s, French and English physicists realized that electricity could travel along wires. They investigated what we call positive and negative charges In 1746, Dutch scientist Pieter van Musschenbroek (1692-1761) invented the

William Herschel's telescope was the world's largest at the time, with a tube almost 40 feet (12 meters) long.

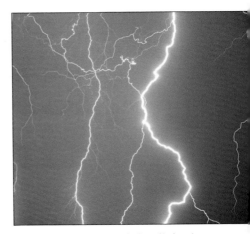

Early people believed that lightning was a sign from the gods. In 1752, Benjamin Franklin examined lightning scientifically.

**Did You Know?**

### COMETS AND PLANETS
- Edmond Halley (1656–1742) figured out the way in which comets orbit the Sun. His theory was proved in spectacular style when a comet appeared in the night sky in 1758, sixteen years after his death—exactly as he predicted.
- In 1781, German-born astronomer William Herschel (1738–1822) used his telescope to discover a new planet—Uranus. His sister, Caroline (1750–1848), was also an astronomer and one of the first great women scientists. She is known for astronomical discoveries of her own.

Leyden jar. This was a glass flask coated inside and outside with metal. It could be used to build up and store electricity. The modern name for a device that works like a Leyden jar is "**capacitor.**"

In 1752, American statesman and scientist Benjamin Franklin (1706–1790) risked his life flying a kite in a thunderstorm. Lightning ran down the wet string and passed along a metal key into a Leyden jar. Franklin's experiment showed that lightning was the same thing as electricity.

Italian Luigi Galvani (1737–1798) opened up another interesting area of research by looking into the effect of electricity on living things. In 1780, he observed electric current passing through the muscles of frogs. He thought that this was part of a biological process, but in this case, the electricity was simply being passed between metals on either side of the frog.

In 1794, Galvani's friend, Alessandro Volta (1745–1827) discovered what was really happening with electricity and the frog muscles. Volta showed that if the frog was taken out of the experiment, electrical current still flowed from one metal to the other. Volta used this discovery to design a device that created electricity by chemical means. He found that when disks (**electrodes**) of zinc and silver were placed in a solution of acid, current flowed along a wire between them. This was the first proper electric battery, invented in 1800.

## Plant Science

New methods and discoveries in chemistry and physics were also helping people understand other sciences, such as botany.

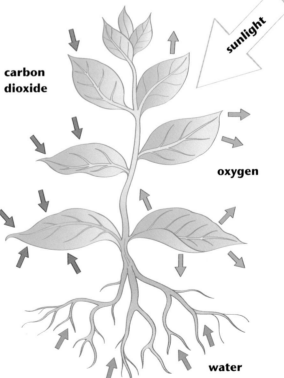

Plants make their own food in a process called photosynthesis. They use sunlight, water, and gases from Earth's atmosphere to grow and produce leaves, seeds, and fruit.

# History of Science

Joseph Priestley also discovered that plants released oxygen into the air. In 1804, scientists finally realized that plants used carbon dioxide from the atmosphere. Dutch scientist Jan Ingenhousz (1730-1799) figured out that plants use the Sun's energy to create food—a process called **photosynthesis**.

## Listing and Naming

By the eighteenth century, knowledge of the natural world was growing fast. Scientists needed a way to put all this information in order. Swedish doctor Carolus Linnaeus (or Carl von Linné, 1707-1778) began grouping similar plants and animals. He gave each animal two Latin names. The first names the **genus** (or type), and the second names the **species** (or exact) name of the animal. This naming process is called **classification**, or taxonomy. Today, all living things have scientific names. Humans belong to the genus *Homo* (human) and the species *sapiens* (wise).

## Farming Science

Often throughout history, the work of scientists has little effect on the daily lives of people. In the 1700s, however, science was offering new ideas and technologies that quickly resulted in huge changes to the way people lived and worked.

For example, farms produced more crops as scientists learned a way for growing crops that maintained the soil's nutrients—the ingredients that make it good for plants. Farms also grew crops more successfully as better machinery was made for plowing fields, sowing seeds, and **threshing** grain. This period of time (1750-1900) was known as the Agricultural Revolution.

## The Birth of Industry

The 1700s introduced better ways of smelting and forging iron, too. In 1709, new furnaces were built in England that used coke (processed coal) rather than charcoal.

New iron-working methods were developed in Sweden in 1745. Iron could now be used to build strong

Classifying animal species helps avoid confusion. The scientific name for this jaguar is *Panthera onca*.

etal bridges, powerful machines, and etter engines.

In 1698, a **steam engine** was invented or pumping water from mine shafts. 1712, English engineer Thomas ewcomen (1663–1729) improved the eam engine design by adding a **pis-on**, and in 1769 James Watt (1736–1819), a Scottish inventor, designed model with a separate **condenser**. oth of these changes made the igine more powerful and efficient. 1770, steam was used to power a iree-wheeled carriage in France. By 783, the first steam-powered boat opeared there, too. Steam engines ould drive all sorts of machinery, ich as looms for weaving cloth.

Many new weaving and spinning iachines were invented in the 700s. In England, new factories egan to produce ironwork, textiles, and pottery. A network of canals was dug to transport the goods. This was the beginning of the Industrial Revolution, the factory age of powered machinery that soon spread across northern Europe and into the northeastern United States.

This miniature working model shows Newcomen's remarkable steam engine.

**A MEDICAL BREAKTHROUGH**
• While in Turkey in 1717, Lady Mary Wortley Montagu (1689–1762) of England noticed that people deliberately infected themselves with a mild form of smallpox disease. Once they caught this mild form of the disease, they usually could not catch the more severe form. She introduced this idea, called variolation, to England in 1721.
• In 1796, English doctor Edward Jenner (1749–1823) used Montagu's idea for preventing disease. He purposedly gave patients a mild form of an illness called cowpox to protect them against smallpox. This practice, called vaccination, is still used today to protect us against a number of diseases.

# CHAPTER 5

# Progress and Industry

In 1800, it was still just about possible for one person to know all there was to know about science. By 1900, human knowledge of the universe, matter, and life had grown so rapidly that one scientist could no longer keep up with all the advances. New branches of science were developing at a breakneck pace.

By this time, as well, many people believed that progress toward a better future depended on science. New museums of natural history and geology opened and botanical gardens and zoos became popular. More students were studying sciences at universities, and some of them were now women.

## Atoms and Molecules

Englishman John Dalton (1766–1844) was one of those early scientists who was inter-

By the mid nineteenth century, natural history museums and botanical gardens were being opened. This photograph shows the U.S. Botanic Garden and the U.S. Capitol in 1865.

ested in all branches of research. He studied weather science (meteorology) all his life and investigated color blindness, from which he suffered. His research into gases made him realize that all the atoms of any one element are exactly the same and have the same **atomic weight**. They can combine with atoms of other elements to form chemical compounds. Chemical changes in a substance were simply the result of the atoms regrouping.

Other chemists added to Dalton's work, helping to clarify the basic structure of substances. Among them was Italian chemist Amedeo Avogadro (1776–1856). His work suggested that elements or compounds contained groups of combined atoms.

These groups are now known as **molecules**. Avogadro's name is still used to describe the constant number of atoms or molecules in one gram of a substance—"Avogadro's number."

## Unknown Elements

In 1869, Russian chemist Dmitri Mendeleyev (1834–1907) drew up a new table of the elements, grouped according t

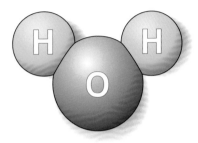

…ch water molecule contains two hydrogen
(H) atoms and one (O) oxygen atom. The
shorthand symbol for water is $H_2O$.

…eir atomic weights. Mendeleyev looked
…the pattern of the table and realized that
…ere seemed to be gaps in the sequence.
…New elements continued to be discov-
…ed. For example, scientists isolated (sepa-
…ated) an element called vanadium in 1869
…d another, called neon, in 1898. As new
…ements were discovered, scientists real-
…ed that each new element fit into the
…ps in the table—just as Mendeleyev
…d forecast. Today, 117 elements are
…own to science, and the existence of
…e more new one has been predicted.

## …lectricity and Magnetism

…eanwhile, interest in electricity continued.
…1820 in Denmark, Hans Christian Ørsted
…777–1851) discovered that an electric

Marie Sklodowska Curie and her husband,
Pierre Curie, isolated the elements radium
and polonium.

current produces a magnetic effect. In
London in 1831, Michael Faraday
(1791–1867) experimented with electromagnetism. Building on Ørsted's idea,
Faraday proposed that since an electric current produces a magnetic field, a magnetic
field might be able to generate an electric
current. The success of his experiments
led to the ability to mechanically produce
electricity and, eventually, the first
electric motor.

## SCIENCE MADE USEFUL

Scientists often come up with practical
inventions as a result of their studies.
In 1815, English scientist Humphry Davy
(1778–1829) invented a safety lamp for
miners to use underground. The safety lamp
reduced the chance of an open flame ignit-
ing gas found in the atomosphere of the
mines. The safety lamp saved many lives.

## Making Waves

Scottish physicist James Clerk Maxwell (1831–1879) studied the mathematics of electromagnetism. He proved that light was made up of electromagnetic **radiation** that traveled in waves. He also believed that there were types of radiation other than light.

In the early 1800s, William Herschel had investigated the possibility of different wavelengths. Maxwell believed that some types of radiation, such as **infrared**, had long **wavelengths**. The longest wavelengths of all belonged to **radio waves**.

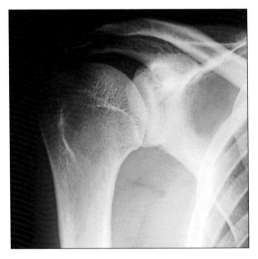

X-rays provide a valuable diagnostic tool and offer treatment options.

German physicist Heinrich Hertz (1857–1894) began studying radio waves in about 1885. In 1895, Wilhelm Roentgen (1845-1923), another German physicist, discovered a kind of high-energy radiation with such a short wavelength that it could pass through human flesh. He called them "X-rays." The first X-ray photograph amazed the world, for it showed very clearly, and rather spookily, the bones of Roentgen's wife's hand.

## Radioactivity

Toward the end of the nineteenth century, a type of radiation given off by elements such as uranium and radium was making news. In France, Henri Becquerel (1852–1908) and Polish-born scientist Marie Sklodowska Curie (1867–1934) and her husband, French scientist Pierre Curie (1859–1906), conducted investigations. In 1897, Marie Curie declared that these elements displayed **radioactivity**. This type of radiation is caused by a gradual breakdown or "decay" in the structure of the atoms making up the elements.

## Inside the Atom

English physicist J. J. Thomson (1856–1940) made an astonishing discovery in 1897:

## MARY HAD A LITTLE . . . FOSSIL?

In 1811, twelve-year-old Mary Anning (1799–1847) discovered a fantastic fossil in Dorset, England. She found the complete skeleton of a prehistoric creature called an ichthyosaur. Anning later discovered plesiosaur and pterodactyl fossils.

oms, which for so long had been
escribed as the smallest possible particle of
atter, actually contained even smaller parti-
es. Thomson called the particles "electrons."
ecause of this discovery, the theory of
oms as the building blocks of the universe
ould need rethinking.

## ife on Earth

ther new ideas included thoughts on
ow life had developed on Earth. In 1801,
founder of France's Natural History
useum, botanist Jean-Baptiste de Lamarck
744–1829), had noticed that many living
eatures and **fossils** shared similar **char-
cteristics**. Lamarck came to believe that
er the ages, simple life-forms become
mplicated ones, and that animals

## NATURAL SELECTION

"I have called this principle, by which each slight variation, is useful, is preserved, by the term of Natural Selection..."

Charles Darwin (1809-1882)

could pass on their characteristics to
future generations.

Two English scientists, Alfred Russel
Wallace (1823–1913) and Charles Darwin
(1809–1882), independently traveled the
world studying and comparing fossils,
plants, and animals. They, too, realized that
life-forms developed and changed over the
ages by a gradual process called **evolution**.

ur modern-day fascination with dinosaurs began with scientific discoveries in the 1800s.

According to Darwin, evolution was not a question of life-forms becoming more complicated. He believed it was a process called **natural selection**. His famous book, *On the Origin of Species by Means of Natural Selection*, appeared in 1859. According to the book, over time, related life-forms change by adapting to the type of environment in which they live. If conditions change and an animal does not adapt, it becomes **extinct**.

The new theories of evolution upset many Christians. They believed that God had made creatures, including humans, in exactly the same form in which they exist today. Christians particularly opposed any idea that apes and humans may have shared common origins. The topic caused noisy public arguments and debates.

## Peas in a Pod

Another important discovery that occurred in the late nineteenth century was hardly noticed. Gregor Mendel (1822–1884), an Austrian monk and botanist, had patiently bred pea plants. While watching plants grow may not seem an exciting way to spend one's days, Mendel's 1866 study of the way that different characteristics pass from one generation to the next was groundbreaking science. It marked the beginnings of a new branch of science known as **genetics**.

In the 1920s, scientists took another look at Mendel's ideas. At that time, they finally realized the value of Mendel's contributions to both botany and genetics.

## Medical Science

Biologists in the 1800s also made great advances in medicine, which soon were saving millions of lives. In 1865, French scientist Louis Pasteur (1822–1895) learned how some types of bacteria can cause diseases. English surgeon Joseph Lister (1827–1912) discovered that dangerous bacteria could be killed by using **antiseptic** chemicals such as carbolic acid. For the first time, surgeons could use a chemical spray to help prevent infections during and after an operation.

## Transportation and Factories

Technology in the 1800s was moving ahead at a faster rate than ever before. New forms of transportation had come into use, including the steam locomotive (1803), the bicycle (1839), and the gas-driven automobile (1885). Large, efficient factories used new machines that did part of the work that was formerly done by hand. Better ways of making steel and glass were invented. Workers left their homes in the countryside for jobs in the rapidly growing cities.

**Louis Pasteur founded the science of microbiology, the study of very small organisms.**

## seful Inventions

ew inventions included photography 822), the sewing machine (1851), artificial es (1856), cellulose (the first plastic (1862), the typewriter (1867), telephones (1876), record-players (1877), and electric lightbulbs (1879). At the time, human cleverness seemed limitless.

his three-wheeler car was designed by German engineer Karl Benz in 1885. The *internal com- ustion engine* that powered this car would change the world.

## ANY COLOR YOU WANT AS LONG AS IT'S MAUVE!

Before 1856, the only way to dye cloth was with natural colors taken from plants, animals (often from their seashells), or minerals. Scientist William Perkin (1838–1907) invented a purple chemical dye, called mauveine. The new color created a fashion sensation, and every young woman wanted a dress in "mauve."

# The Twentieth Centur

"Modern" has become a favorite word over the last one hundred years or so. People love things that are new and different. In the 1900s, there was no shortage of new discoveries. It seemed that many human dreams from across the ages were at last coming true.

## New Technologies

In the 1900s, new materials such as plastics and nylon came into use. Factories turned out cars, preserved foods, and offered ready-made clothes. The first plane flew in 1903, and by 1969, men walked on the Moon. This was the age when radio, talking movies, television, refrigerators, air conditioners, sky-scrapers, rockets, and submarines became common. Everyday life became faster and more frantic.

Even so, people began having nagging doubts about science and technology. Scientific research was creating terrible new weapons, such as military tanks, poison gas, and bombs. Mineral mining began using up Earth's riches at alarming rates. The effects of technology and transportation were **polluting** air, land, and sea. Science and technology became more important and powerful, and scientists often faced difficult decisions.

## Understanding Energy

Science produced many shocking new ideas at the start of the century. Even the important theories of Isaac Newton were

The search for oil in the U.S. began in the 1930s. In this picture from 1944, oil derric crowd the Californian coastline.

examined. In 1900, German physicist Max Planck (1858–1947) showed that energy is not continuous. That means it does not flow smoothly like a stream does. Energy, Planck said, moves, or is radiated, as a series of small bursts. He called these bursts quanta. This act—how energy flows—affects the behavior of atoms and molecules.

In 1911, New Zealander Ernest Rutherford (1871–1937) suggested that atoms had a powerful central core or **nucleus**, which was about ten thousand times smaller than the atom. The electrons, he said, whizzed around this nucleus. In the years that followed, two more types of tiny particles were identified within the atom. These were called protons and neutrons.

Astronauts first walked on the Moon in July 1969.

matics of movement, light, time, and the way in which the universe works.

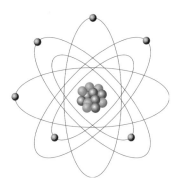

The determination of the structure of the atom was one of the most important discoveries of the twentieth century.

### Einstein's World

The greatest genius of the modern age was German-born scientist Albert Einstein (1879–1955). Einstein studied the mathe-

## Q&A   HOW IS AN ATOM LIKE THE SOLAR SYSTEM?

In 1907, J. J. Thomson suggested that electrons were arranged randomly around an atom's nucleus. In somewhat the same way, the planets of our solar system orbit the Sun. Unlike the planets, however, an electron could orbit virtually anywhere around the outside of the nucleus. (The planets follow a set orbit around the Sun in basically the same plane at all times.)

Alexander Fleming's discovery of penicillin led to the development of other antibiotics—one of the greatest advances in the history of medicine.

## Relativity

Einstein based his theories on the idea of **relativity**. In other words, in a universe that is full of motion, movement can only be described in relation to (how it behaves in the presence of) other objects. For example, you may seem to be completely motionless in relation to (compared to) your chair, but in reality, you are shooting through space along with your chair and the rest of the planet. Incredibly, even the values for time and mass are not stable, said Einstein. Time and mass can vary according to the motion of the person measuring them. Einstein believed that the only thing that remains the same is the speed of light.

## Mass and Energy

Einstein also understood that mass and energy are different forms of the same thing. In 1939, scientists discovered how to split the unsplittable—the nucleus of an atom. Just as earlier physicists predicted, matter changed into an enormous burst of energy in the process, called **nuclear fission**.

## Q&A

### HOW CAN IT KILL *AND* CURE??

Researchers discovered early in the 1900s that radioactive substances can cause terrible illnesses, such as cancer. By careful use in measured doses, however, radiation can also kill off cancerous growths. By the 1930s, "radiation therapy" was saving lives.

1945, bombs powered by nuclear fission ere used to end World War II. Einstein and ther nuclear physicists spent much of their me campaigning for world peace. By 1954, eaceful uses of nuclear fission provided e power to generate electricity.

## ttacking Germs

ther scientific discoveries saved life rather an destroying it. Among the most impor- nt medical discoveries of e century were new ugs called **antibiotics**. ver since Louis Pasteur id learned about harmful icteria, scientists had en looking for new ays of attacking these nwelcome organisms. Yet accident led to peni- lin, the first antibiotic.

In 1928, Scottish sur- on Alexander Fleming 881–1955) left bacteria a laboratory dish while was away. When he turned, he found that e samples had gotten oldy. As he was about throw out the samples, noticed that one of e molds had prevented me of the bacteria from owing.

Fleming realized that is mold could be used to kill bacteria (germs), and from it he cre- ated penicillin. No one realized the full effect of penicillin until the 1930s. Then, two scientists, Australian Howard Florey (1898–1968) and German-born Ernst Chain (1906–1979) teamed up to study penicillin. By 1943, penicillin was being manufactured in the United States and used for destroying diseases and fighting infections.

**Albert Einstein's Theory of Relativity changed our understanding of time, motion, and the universe.**

# History of Science

## Secrets of Life

One of the greatest mysteries of modern science continued to baffle scientists since Gregor Mendel first launched his genetic studies. Just how are characteristics passed from parent to child? Scientists discovered that the cell, the basic building block of all living matter, contained units of heredity called **genes**. Genes determine whether a baby has black hair, blue eyes, and straight teeth. Genes are made of a chemical called deoxyribonucleic acid. Scientists simply call it **DNA**!

The structure of DNA was baffling to scientists in the 1950s. It took the work of several people to solve the puzzle. British scientists Rosalind Franklin (1920–1958) and Maurice Wilkins (1916–2004) examined countless X-ray images. Another British scientist, Francis Crick (1916–2004) and U.S. scientist James Watson (b. 1928) swapped ideas and hunches. They finally cracked the structure mystery. The DNA molecule was shown to have the shape of a double **helix**—like a twisted ladder. At last, one of the great secrets of life was revealed!

## A Space Age

The twentieth century was the age of fantastic space discoveries. In 1929, American astronomer Edwin Hubble (1889–1953) proved the existence of many galaxies other than our own. And, he noted nearly all of these other galaxies were speeding away from our solar system at a rate known as the "Hubble Constant." That surely meant that the universe was expanding. So how had it started? Some scientists proposed that it began with a giant explo-

The double-helix structure of DNA, shown in this model, was the most important discovery in the history of genetics.

he miniaturization of components allowed
r the development of powerful computers.

on. This theory, known as the "**big bang**,"
just one of many scientists still debate.

During the twentieth century,
ore telescopes began explor-
g the universe using radio,
frared, and other wavelengths,
addition to visible light.

Space exploration started in
957 with the launch of *Sputnik*
what is now Russia.

Satellites are natural or man-
ade objects that revolve
ound a planet. Since *Sputnik*,
any **space probes** have been
nt out by various nations to
plore the solar system.

## The Computer Age

During the 1940s, U.S. and British universities developed an invention that would
completely change the work of scientists,
mathematicians, and, in time, the entire
world. It was the electronic computer.
The first computers were huge, heavy,
slow machines.

Then, in 1969, the silicon chip was developed in the United States. Although tiny, this
**microprocessor** was able to handle even
complicated **circuits**. In 1975, home computers began appearing in the United States.
Since then, the chip has become ever more
compact and powerful. It can be used for all
sorts of jobs, such as storing
data, calculating, and testing
theories in the business
world. Television, radio, and
music industries all depend
on the chip. In the 1980s
and 1990s, scientists developed global computer net-
works. The Internet provided
instant worldwide communi-
cations by computer, while
the World Wide Web provided access to an enormous
range of information.

The launch of *Sputnik*
caused enormous contro-
versy around the world.

# DON'T BLINK!

In 1916, German physicist Karl
Schwarzschild (1873–1916) determined
the theory of black holes. Black holes are
objects in space that have such a strong
gravitational pull that they suck in all
matter around them—even light. Black
holes cannot be seen, but their effects
can be recorded.

# CHAPTER 7

# Present and Future

In the 2000s, scientists know more about Earth and the universe than ever before. The more we learn, however, the more questions arise. Many challenges lie ahead. For example, many people in the world are poor, have little food, and lack clean water. Diseases such as malaria, tuberculosis, or AIDS still cause countless deaths worldwide and create new medical challenges. The work of a scientist who designs a simple stove may prove just as important as the scientific work that goes into developing a new computer software or a new spacecraft.

## Journeys into Space

The *Hubble Space Telescope* (*HST*), launched by the United States in 1990, orbits Earth as it scans the farthest reaches of the universe. Clear of Earth's atmosphere, the *HST* has sent back amazing images of stars being born and of distant galaxies. Another powerful new telescope, the infrared *James Webb Space Telescope*, will soon join the *HST* in space. It is set for launch in 2013.

Meanwhile, scientists from North America, Europe, and Asia continue working on new series of spacecraft to explore the planets and to possibly land on the Moon. Will humans eventually travel to distant planets and settle in new worlds? Will they be able to travel through time? Science often catches up with people's wildest dreams, but it is impossible to say if and when this might happen.

## Meanwhile Back on Earth . . .

Every part of Earth's surface can now be mapped from space. Although areas of the ocean still need exploring, we now have images

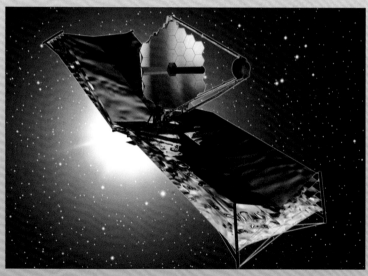

NASA's *James Webb Space Telescope* will explore the universe using infrared radiation.

With the global population topping 6.5 billion, pressure on our planet's resources increases daily. Some running events help support organizations that distribute food.

f the deepest ocean floor, a mysterious ealm where molten rock bursts through om deep inside the planet and cools to orm new rock. We understand the behavior f Earth's crust, and, from space, we can ven measure the slow movements of the ontinents and ocean currents.

## Crowded World

/e know our planet better than ever efore, but that is not to say we understand ow to treat it wisely. How many people can live comfortably on Earth? As of 2006, the population has passed 6,500,000,000. By 2050, it could be 9,225,000,000.

Every day, our growing population needs more food, more electricity, and more fuel. Our needs destroy the natural environment, including the world's forests—which supply life-sustaining oxygen.

Many scientists today work to ensure that we do not take from Earth more than we can give back. This balance is called **sustainability**.

## SUPERCRASH!

• The world's largest atomic particle research facility is CERN, located underground on the French-Swiss border in a 17 mile-long (27 km) tunnel. CERN's latest super-machine, called the Large Hadron Collider (or LHC), is planned to begin operating in 2007. A collider smashes together atoms almost at the speed of light, in order to study the particles that are given out.

(Note: The name CERN comes from the French *Conseil Européen pour la Recherche Nucléaire*, or the European Council for Nuclear Research.)

• Scientists at CERN invented the World Wide Web.

## Energy and Climate

Earth is kept warm by infrared radiation from the Sun as well as that given off by Earth itself. The heat that gets trapped in gases in the atmosphere creates what is called the "greenhouse effect." Many scientists believe that invisible gases from cars, aircraft, and factories are making this effect more extreme, causing global warming—a rapid rise in global temperatures. Global warming could increase the spread of deserts, promote more occurrences of violent weather such as hurricanes, and cause a rise in global sea levels as ice melts from around the polar areas. Dealing with global warming is one of the biggest problems facing people living in the twenty-first century.

The use of oil, gas, or coal for power or fuel makes this problem worse. These substances are called fossil fuels, because they come from the remains of prehistoric sources of carbon such as trees, plants, and animals.

One way to reduce the greenhouse effect is to find practical ways of capturing and storing the carbon that these fuels push out into the atmosphere in the form of gases.

Another way is to develop more renewable forms of energy. This means using carbon-free sources of energy that do not run out and do not need replacing. Wind, tides, waves, and **sola** (Sun) power are all examples of renewable energy.

In the future, single houses may be able to generate all their own power using some of these methods, instead of relying on energy from a power plant. Another way of fighting global warming is to save or conserve energy, so that we use less of it in the first place.

Humanity's future may depend on scientific research into deadly diseases such as AIDS.

## GLOBAL WARMING

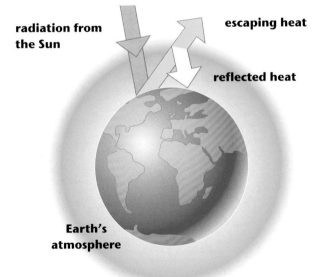

**radiation from the Sun**

**escaping heat**

**reflected heat**

**Earth's atmosphere**

More heat than usual is being trapped by gases in Earth's atmosphere. This process, called global warming, leads to changing weather patterns around the world.

## HOT STUFF

Even a small increase in worldwide ocean temperatures will greatly change the world as we know it.

If the Antarctic and Artic ice caps keep melting at the present rate, Earth will experience an increased loss of plant and animal species. Huge storms that cause severe damage will also occur more frequently.

ectronic technology, like this camera cell phone, is rapidly changing our lives. Advanced chnology affects scientific research methods as well as everyday activities.

## Making Connectionss

Electronics are advancing at high speed. Computers, cell phones, radio, television, photography, and many other technologies are already overlapping. We can take photographs with a telephone and download music from our computers. Soon, all the machines we use to run our daily lives will be linked and networked.

These piglets were created by cloning. What paths should genetic research take in the twenty-first century?

## Genes and Clones

Scientists continue to discover new facts about genes and **inheritance**. By experimenting with genes, scientists hope to bring an end to inherited diseases.

The genes of many plants have been altered or modified in an attempt to produce plants that are supposedly better than the originals, perhaps better able to withstand disease or drought. Many scientists say this **genetic modification (GM)** is not all that different from traditional breeding methods. Others fear that GM crops may escape into the wild and affect natural plant and animal life.

In 1996, Scottish scientists cloned a sheep, taking cells from the mother to create a genetically identical lamb named "Dolly." Some scientists want to **clone** creatures to produce "perfect" farm animals, to

provide medical cures, or to produce pets. Human cloning methods have not been successful and are outlawed in many countries. Among other ethical concerns, many people worry that genetic engineering will upset the natural balance of life on Earth.

## As Small As It Gets . . .

The miniaturization that has taken place in the world of electronics is nothing compared to new areas of scientific research called **nanotechnologies**. These aim to build structures at the unbelievably small scale of molecules or atoms in order to create new materials. They may be useful in manufacturing fibers, medicines, and many other goods. Some people fear that entirely new materials accidentally released into the environment may cause unforeen and potentially harmful reactions in ur natural world.

### ight or Wrong?

ew questions constantly arise for scien-sts. Many companies already "own" a mod-ied gene or matter created by nanotech-ology. Is that "right"? Should weapons of ass destruction be allowed into space? ow much should governments control hat scientists are allowed to do?

Scientists of today should take note of e past. Efforts designed to "conquer" ature are often disastrous. Science and chnology meant to work with nature d the planet will likely prove useful to human survival. The history of science shows that the human spirit is one of curiosity, inventiveness, and desire for the truth. The Greeks created the word "*phi-losophy.*" Do you remember what that means? A love of wisdom—may we use this knowledge well.

## QUESTIONS, QUESTIONS

"Learn from yesterday, live for today, hope for tomorrow. The important thing is not to stop questioning."

Albert Einstein (1879-1955)

rotesters act against GM (genetic modification) by disrupting a trial planting of genetically nodified crops. Scientific advancements have often faced social and political controversies.

**accelerate**  to go faster; to gather speed

**acid**  one of a group of substances containing hydrogen, which usually has a sharp, sour taste

**alchemy**  a false science that was the forerunner of chemistry

**algebra**  a branch of mathematics that shows relationships, using letters, numbers, and other symbols

**alkali**  one of a group of substances that neutralize acids and form salts

**alloy**  a mixture of metals

**amber**  a fossilized plant resin, generally colored yellow or brown

**anatomy**  the study of the structure of living things, especially the human body

**antibiotic**  a medicine based upon organisms that attack or kill certain bacteria

**antiseptic**  a chemical that destroys bacteria or germs

**astronomy**  the scientific study of space, including stars, planets, moons, comets, and black holes

**atmosphere**  the layer of gases that surrounds a planet such as Earth

**atom**  the smallest single part of an element, containing tiny particles around a central nucleus

**atomic weight**  the average weight of atoms in any given sample of an element

**bacteria**  small, simple organisms, some of which (germs) can cause disease

**big bang theory**  a theory that the universe started with a massive explosion of matter

**botany**  the scientific study of plants

**capacitor**  a device for building up and storing an electric charge

**cell**  one of the tiny units that make up the structure of all living things

**characteristics**  physical traits

**circuit**  the complete path followed by an electric current

**classification**  any systematic grouping, especially of living things

**cloning**  reproducing a new plant or animal from an existing cell rather than by sexual reproduction

**combustion**  burning, rapidly combining a substance with oxygen and so creating light and heat

**condenser**  an apparatus for condensing gas or vapor

**constellation**  an apparent pattern of stars in the sky, as seen from Earth

**diagnosis**  conclusions drawn from the scientific examination of a sick person

**displace**  to take the place of

**DNA**  deoxyribonucleic acid, a chemical that occurs naturally in living cells and transfers certain characteristics from one generation to the next

**drought**  a prolonged period marked by a lack of rainfall

**eclipse**  the blocking of light by the movement of planets or moons, as when the Moon comes between the Sun and Earth, or when the Moon falls within the shadow of Earth

**electrode**  a metal or other substance that conducts electricity into or out of a battery

**element**  any basic substance made up of identical atoms, not mixed with others as in a compound

**elliptical**  oval, shaped like a flattened-out circle

**evidence**  facts that prove or disprove a theory

**evolution**  the gradual change and development of life forms

**extinct**  of a species that has died out

**fossil**  the remains or trace of prehistoric animal or plants, preserved in stone

**galaxy**  any large system of stars held together in space by gravity

**gene**  a unit of inheritance, found within the cells of all life forms

**genetics**  the science of genes and how they pass on characteristics from one generation to another

**genus** a group of related species within a "family" of plants or animals

**geometry** the branch of mathematics that deals with shapes and areas

**genetic modification** (GM), changing the make-up of the genes within a life form

**gravity** the force of attraction between two objects (such as the force between a planet and bodies near it)

**helix** a spiral or screw shape

**immortal** a person that lives forever

**inheritance** the way characteristics are passed down from parent to child

**infrared** rays with a longer wavelength than light

**magnetism** the force that attracts or repels substances such as iron

**mass** the amount of matter within a substance

**microprocessor** the miniaturized processing unit in a computer

**microscope** any instrument with lenses that uses light or beams of electrons to magnify very small objects

**mineral** any substance that is commonly mined, such as metal ores, stones, and rocks, or coal

**molecule** the tiniest unit that displays all the characteristics of a substance

**myth** a traditional story, often used to explain the natural world in terms of supernatural events, gods, spirits, animals, and heroes

**natural selection** the process that guides evolution by favoring the characteristics of an organism that ensures its survival as a species

**nanotechnology** the manipulation of atoms or molecules to create new substances and materials

**nuclear fission** the splitting of a heavy atomic nucleus, such as uranium, resulting in the release of huge amounts of energy

**nucleus** the central part or core of something, around which other things are grouped, as inside an atom

**nutrient** a substance that provides nourishment or food for living things

**observatory** a place or building designed for viewing and studying the stars, planets, and the other bodies in space

**optics** the science of light and sight

**ore** rocks that contain metals

**pendulum** a weighted rod that swings to and fro, affected by gravity and momentum

**philosophy** the study of knowledge, truth, and ideas

**phlogiston** a chemical once believed to be released during combustion. Phlogiston does not exist.

**photosynthesis** the way in which plants use sunlight to convert water and carbon dioxide into food

**piston** a moving disc or cylinder fitted inside a tube and pushed back and forth by pressure, used to move a rod up and down

**pollute** to poison air, land, or water with waste chemicals

**prism** a transparent piece of glass, generally triangular, that breaks up light into the colors of the rainbow.

**radiation** the process of giving out of rays, such as light, heat, or radioactivity

**radioactivity** a type of radiation given out by some elements whose atoms are in a state of decay

**radio waves** a form of radiation with a wavelength longer than infrared

**reason** the use of clear, logical thought

**refract** to change the direction of a ray of light

**relativity** the theory that motion can be measured only in relation to the motion of another object

**resistance** the way in which one object or force opposes another, as when an aircraft is resisted by air

**ritual** a religious ceremony

**satellite** 1) a body that orbits a larger one, such as a moon going around a planet; 2) a spacecraft designed to orbit a natural body such as a planet or moon

**smelt** to remove a metal from ore by heating it until it is molten

**solar** to do with the Sun

**space probe** a spacecraft, without human crew, designed to explore space

**species** a single type of animal or plant. The ostrich is a species of bird.

**steam engine** a stationary engine driven or worked by steam

**superstition** a belief that is not based on reason

**survey** to measure land or buildings

**sustainability** a balance, as of a system or an environment, in which care is taken to maintain resources by taking no more than one puts in

**symptom** a sign of illness

**technology** practical uses of science, such as engineering or industry

**threshing** separating out the grain from a crop by beating

**universe** all of space and everything it contains

**wavelength** in electromagnetic radiation, the distance from the crest of one wave to the crest of the next

# FURTHER INFORMATION

## Books

Bankston, John. *Francis Crick and James Watson: Pioneers in DNA Research Unlocking the Secrets of Science.* Mitchell Lane Publishers (2002).

Delano, Marfe Ferguson. *Genius: A Photobiography of Albert Einstein.* National Geographic (2005).

Ingram, Scott. *Nicolaus Copernicus.* Giants of Science (series). Blackbirch Press (2004).

Kjelle, Marylou Morano. *Antoine Lavoisier: Father of Modern Chemistry.* Uncharted, Unexplored, and Unexplained: Science Advancements of the 19th Century (series). Lane (2005).

Steele, Philip. *Galileo: The Genius Who Faced the Inquisition.* NG World History Biographies (series) National Geographic (2005).

# Books (cont.)

Steele, Philip.
*Marie Curie: The Woman who Changed the Course of Science.*
DG World History Biographies (series).
National Geographic (2006).

Wiese, Jim.
*40 Time-Traveling, World-Exploring, History-Making Activities for Kids.*
Ancient Science (series).
Jossey-Bass (2003).

# Web sites

**About Darwin**
www.aboutdarwin.com/index.html
A Web site dedicated to the life and times of Charles Darwin

**Marie Curie — Her Story in Brief**
www.aip.org/history/curie/brief/index.html
Biography of Marie Curie

**Al Dokkan**
www.aldokkan.com/science/science.htm
Egyptian ancient science

**History of Chemistry**
www.columbia.edu/itc/chemistry/chem-2507/navbar/chemhist.html
A timetable of key events in the study of chemistry

**Roman Scientific Achievements**
www.historyforkids.org/learn/romans/science/index.htm

**Indian Scientific Achievements**
www.historyforkids.org/learn/india/science/index.htm

**Medieval Scientific Achievements**
www.historyforkids.org/learn/medieval/science/

**Wesrt Asian Scientific Achievements**
www.historyforkids.org/learn/westasia/science/index.htm

**Albert Einstein Home Page**
www.humboldt1.com/~gralsto/einstein/einstein.html